Best All 'Round

by Marsha Lee Sheiness

A Samuel French Acting Edition

SAMUELFRENCH.COM

Copyright © 1980, 2012 by Marsha Lee Sheiness

ALL RIGHTS RESERVED

CAUTION: Professionals and amateurs are hereby warned that *BEST ALL 'ROUND* is subject to a licensing fee. It is fully protected under the copyright laws of the United States of America, the British Commonwealth, including Canada, and all other countries of the Copyright Union. All rights, including professional, amateur, motion picture, recitation, lecturing, public reading, radio broadcasting, television and the rights of translation into foreign languages are strictly reserved. In its present form the play is dedicated to the reading public only.

The amateur and professional live stage performance rights to *BEST ALL 'ROUND* are controlled exclusively by Samuel French, Inc., and licensing arrangements and performance licenses must be secured well in advance of presentation. PLEASE NOTE that amateur licensing fees are set upon application in accordance with your producing circumstances. When applying for a licensing quotation and a performance license please give us the number of performances intended, dates of production, your seating capacity and admission fee. Licensing fees are payable one week before the opening performance of the play to Samuel French, Inc., at 45 W. 25th Street, New York, NY 10010.

Licensing fee of the required amount must be paid whether the play is presented for charity or gain and whether or not admission is charged.

Professional/Stock licensing fees quoted upon application to Samuel French, Inc.

For all other rights than those stipulated above, apply to: Samuel French, Inc., at 45 W. 25th Street, New York, NY 10010.

Particular emphasis is laid on the question of amateur or professional readings, permission and terms for which must be secured in writing from Samuel French, Inc.

Copying from this book in whole or in part is strictly forbidden by law, and the right of performance is not transferable.

Whenever the play is produced the following notice must appear on all programs, printing and advertising for the play: "Produced by special arrangement with Samuel French, Inc."

Due authorship credit must be given on all programs, printing and advertising for the play.

ISBN 978-0-87440-799-0   Printed in U.S.A.   #B2573

No one shall commit or authorize any act or omission by which the copyright of, or the right to copyright, this play may be impaired.

No one shall make any changes in this play for the purpose of production.

Publication of this play does not imply availability for performance. Both amateurs and professionals considering a production are strongly advised in their own interests to apply to Samuel French, Inc., for written permission before starting rehearsals, advertising, or booking a theatre.

No part of this book may be reproduced, stored in a retrieval system, or transmitted in any form, by any means, now known or yet to be invented, including mechanical, electronic, photocopying, recording, videotaping, or otherwise, without the prior written permission of the publisher.

MUSIC USE NOTE

Licensees are solely responsible for obtaining formal written permission from copyright owners to use copyrighted music in the performance of this play and are strongly cautioned to do so. If no such permission is obtained by the licensee, then the licensee must use only original music that the licensee owns and controls. Licensees are solely responsible and liable for all music clearances and shall indemnify the copyright owners of the play and their licensing agent, Samuel French, Inc., against any costs, expenses, losses and liabilities arising from the use of music by licensees.

IMPORTANT BILLING AND CREDIT REQUIREMENTS

All producers of *BEST ALL 'ROUND* must give credit to the Author of the Play in all programs distributed in connection with performances of the Play, and in all instances in which the title of the Play appears for the purposes of advertising, publicizing or otherwise exploiting the Play and/or a production. The name of the Author *must* appear on a separate line on which no other name appears, immediately following the title and *must* appear in size of type not less than fifty percent of the size of the title type.

BEST ALL 'ROUND was first presented by The Prism Theater at the Perry Street Theater in New York City. The performance was directed by Stephen Stewart-James, with sets by Patrick Mann, costumes by Sam Fleming, and sound by Eloida G. Hulbert. The Production Stage Manager was Susanne Jul. The cast was as follows:

MICHAEL LEE	Nina Levine
NICKIE	Lisa Reed
KAY	Lisa Kable
VOICE OF ROSY	Mary Caton

CHARACTERS

MICHAEL LEE GOODMAN - 17 years old
SUSAN NICKIE - 17 years old
KAY GOODMAN - 11 years old
ROSY'S VOICE - 18 years old

SETTING

South Texas

TIME

1958

SET

One set – 2 locations
(Second location can be accomplished simply with lights and sound.)

*Dedicated to my sister,
Diana Kay Sheiness*

ACT ONE

(Late afternoon. **MICHAEL GOODMAN***'s bedroom. She and her best friend,* **SUSAN NICKIE** *are listening to the 50s rock tune,* Rock with Me Henry*. *Both feel the beat while working algebra problems and trading answers.)*

MICHAEL. Okay, I finished another one. How are you doing? *(hands* **NICKIE** *her paper)*

NICKIE. *(taking paper and copying answer)* Algebra is for the birds.

MICHAEL. Don't I know it? *(sings along with the record)*

NICKIE. Spare me, Goodman. I can't concentrate with that going on.

MICHAEL. *(a little hurt)* Okay. *(Goes back to algebra. The phone rings.* **MICHAEL** *screams.)* It's him!! I told you he'd call here.

NICKIE. Don't answer it. Let it ring a few times.

MICHAEL. Maybe it's my mother.

NICKIE. So? You're going to answer it.

MICHAEL. When?

NICKIE. Right – now!!

*(***MICHAEL** *answers the phone.)*

MICHAEL. Hello. – Hi, Grady. Just a minute. *(breathless with excitement – to* **NICKIE***)* It's him. What'll I say? Do you want to talk to him?

NICKIE. Did he ask to speak to me?

MICHAEL. Why else do you think he called?

NICKIE. Tell him I'm not here yet.

---

*See Music Use Note on page 3

MICHAEL. She's not here yet. She is not. That was somebody else. It was my sister, Kay. –Grady, she's not here! –He doesn't believe me.

NICKIE. Oh, all right. *(takes phone)* Grady? Hi. I just got here. – I told you I can't. – Because I'm studying algebra with Michael. I have to; we have a test tomorrow. You want to come over and study?

MICHAEL. Oh, no!!

NICKIE. Okay, then I'll see you tomorrow in homeroom. *(hangs up)* God, he's in love with me. One date and he wants to marry me, practically.

MICHAEL. I could just die. Grady Van Vleck. Most Handsome and star quarterback. I could die.

NICKIE. So could I. But I don't want to marry him.

MICHAEL. Did he really ask you to marry him?

NICKIE. Not in so many words.

MICHAEL. Is he coming over here? I hope not.

NICKIE. He hates to study. I knew he'd say no.

MICHAEL. I couldn't believe you asked him over.

NICKIE. Don't bust a gut. He's not coming.

MICHAEL. Do you want another coke?

NICKIE. I'm bored. Let's go for a drive.

MICHAEL. What about the test tomorrow?

NICKIE. What about it? We'll do okay.

MICHAEL. But I don't understand algebra.

NICKIE. Who does? We can cheat in class, you know. We've done it before.

MICHAEL. I know, but it makes me sick to my stomach.

NICKIE. Let's face it, if Mrs. G doesn't know we're cheating then I'm a toad.

MICHAEL. You're kidding. She *doesn't* know.

NICKIE. She does too. And if she cared, she would have said something by now.

MICHAEL. Maybe you're right – she doesn't even look up during the test.

NICKIE. That's exactly my point. She just sits there and reads her magazines. If you ask me she's just telling us to go ahead and cheat.

MICHAEL. Where did you want to go?

NICKIE. I don't know. Grady said he was going to meet Butch and Dudley at Piks. He said he'd buy us a beer.

MICHAEL. How can he do that? He's under age.

NICKIE. I didn't ask. Come on. We can always come back and study.

MICHAEL. You go ahead. I want to graduate this year.

NICKIE. Oh, all right. God, Goodman, you're so goody, goody all of a sudden.

MICHAEL. I am not! I told you. Cheating makes me sick to my stomach. I can't help it.

NICKIE. Forget it. How many more problems do we have to do?

MICHAEL. Nine.

NICKIE. NINE?!! NINE EACH?

MICHAEL. No, nine in all.

NICKIE. Well, why didn't you say so?

MICHAEL. Nine in all. How could it be nine each? There are only thirteen problems.

NICKIE. I didn't count them.

MICHAEL. Well there's only thirteen in all and there's nine left.

NICKIE. How long will it take us to do nine more?

MICHAEL. I don't know. How long did it take us to do four?

NICKIE. Where's your brainy sister?

MICHAEL. She's only in the eighth grade.

NICKIE. You're always talking about how smart she is.

MICHAEL. She is. Look, if you want to go and meet Grady, go ahead.

NICKIE. I didn't say I wanted to meet him. I just said he was going to be there. I'm not exactly wearing his cleat, you know.

MICHAEL. Did he ask you?

NICKIE. Twice. But I told him that I wasn't ready to go steady with anyone yet. I mean, give me a minute to breathe. I just broke up with Floyd.

MICHAEL. What did he say to that?

NICKIE. Are you crazy? I didn't tell him that. I told him I'd think about it.

MICHAEL. No wonder he called you here.

NICKIE. Aren't you hungry? We could drive over to Piks. Get a hamburger –

MICHAEL. And cheat on the test tomorrow. No!

NICKIE. I don't see what your problem is? Everybody else is going to do it.

MICHAEL. It's not that I don't want to, I can't.

NICKIE. Can I borrow your car? Mine's low on gas.

MICHAEL. How long will you be gone?

NICKIE. I don't know. Where are the keys?

MICHAEL. Okay. But only half an hour. *(hands her the keys)*

NICKIE. I never drove your car. How's the pickup?

MICHAEL. Don't drag anybody. It's not a standard shift.

NICKIE. I'm just going to get myself a hamburger. You want me to bring you back one?

MICHAEL. Okay. And an order of French fries, and a malt. Chocolate.

NICKIE. What time is it? I don't want to be gone more than a half hour.

MICHAEL. Don't speed either.

NICKIE. You want to drive me over there?

MICHAEL. I have to study.

NICKIE. I won't feel guilty if you work out a few of mine while I'm gone.

MICHAEL. It's going to take me forever just to do mine.

NICKIE. Well, if your brainy sister comes home, maybe you could get her to look at them.

MICHAEL. Your time's running out.

NICKIE. I'll be right back.

(She exits.)

*(****MICHAEL*** *goes to record player, puts on* Too Pooped to Pop* *and begins to mime the words. She really gets into it.* ***KAY****, her younger sister enters.* ***KAY*** *is very depressed. She watches* ***MICHAEL****'s lips intently.* ***MICHAEL*** *performs for* ***KAY****.)*

MICHAEL. How was it?

KAY. Okay, I guess.

MICHAEL. It can't be just okay. It's got to be perfect.

KAY. It looked okay to me.

MICHAEL. Are you sure?

KAY. I think so.

MICHAEL. If you don't tell me I'm off, how can I know it?

KAY. I said it looked okay to me.

MICHAEL. Is something the matter?

KAY. What could be the matter?

MICHAEL. I don't know. You're acting like something's the matter.

KAY. Just because I said it looks okay?

MICHAEL. What happened?

KAY. Do you mind? I don't want to talk about it. What are you studying?

MICHAEL. Algebra. Barf!

KAY. Let's see. *(She gives one of the problems a brief depressed look.)* Right. Algebra.

MICHAEL. Do you know how to do this?

KAY. I don't know. I think so.

MICHAEL. You want to help me?

KAY. I'm too tired.

MICHAEL. Okay.

KAY. Your car's stolen. I saw someone driving off in it.

MICHAEL. Nickie borrowed it.

---

*See Music Use Note on page 3

KAY. You better not tell Mom.

MICHAEL. She promised to get back before Mom gets home.

KAY. I wish I could drive.

MICHAEL. You want me to teach you?

KAY. I'm too young to get my license.

MICHAEL. I know, but I still could teach you.

KAY. That would make me more depressed. I would know how to drive, but I wouldn't be allowed to.

MICHAEL. You're right. I won't teach you.

KAY. Maybe next year. You want me to work one of those problems for you?

MICHAEL. That would be fantastic. Do you think you can?

KAY. Let me have the book. I'll try.

MICHAEL. Do you mind if I practice my record?

KAY. What are you practicing for?

MICHAEL. Young Judea's having a dance and I'm part of the entertainment.

KAY. I thought you told me you hated Young Judea dances.

MICHAEL. I do. Nobody ever asks me to dance.

KAY. Then why are you going?

MICHAEL. Because Rodney Goldstein asked me to do one of my pantomimes.

KAY. That's why you're going? To do your pantomime.

MICHAEL. I wish I could come home after that. It's so depressing!

KAY. So why can't you? I would if it were me.

MICHAEL. Easier said than done.

KAY. So?

MICHAEL. So? I'd like to see you do it.

KAY. I'm not even going. I'm never going to one of those depressing dances.

MICHAEL. That's what you think.

KAY. That's what I know.

MICHAEL. If Mom has anything to say about it!

KAY. I'll jut tell her I don't want to go.

MICHAEL. I already tried that. It doesn't work.

KAY. It doesn't work for you. But it's going to work for me.

MICHAEL. How is that going to happen?

KAY. Because *everybody* gets to tell you what to do.

MICHAEL. They do not.

KAY. They do so.

MICHAEL. Like who? Name one person.

KAY. Like Mom!

MICHAEL. That doesn't count!

KAY. Okay. Like Nickie for instance.

MICHAEL. She does not!

KAY. Everyday!

MICHAEL. Then why didn't I go to Piks with her?

KAY. Good question. Why didn't you?

MICHAEL. Because I have to study. That's why!

KAY. So? There's an exception to every rule.

MICHAEL. You're a big help.

KAY. It's not my fault you have to go to those stupid dances.

MICHAEL. I didn't say it was.

KAY. But you're acting like it is.

MICHAEL. All I said was I'm going to do one of my pantomimes at a Young Judea dance, and you end up telling me that everybody gets to tell me what to do. How would you feel if somebody told you something like that?

KAY. Terrible!

MICHAEL. Okay!!

KAY. Okay. I'm sorry. You could pretend you were sick or something though.

MICHAEL. How can I do that if I'm supposed to entertain everybody?

KAY. Why do you want to entertain people who don't want to dance with you?

MICHAEL. What a stupid question.

KAY. I don't think it's so stupid. I mean, what is it? You want everyone to like you?

MICHAEL. Just because I want to do my pantomime?

KAY. I just asked.

MICHAEL. I can't believe you asked such a stupid question.

KAY. I guess you don't want me to help you with your algebra problems anymore.

MICHAEL. You probably don't know how to work them anyway.

KAY. *(reads from algebra book)* 'In dividing one fraction by another, first invert the divisor and then multiply the dividend by the inverted divisor. If the numerator and denominators are written in factored form the result may be simplified by dividing the numerators and denominators by common factors.' – No sweat.

(She works out the problem on paper as **MICHAEL** *puts* Too Pooped to Pop* *on the record player and begins to pantomime to it.)*

(The phone rings. It rings at least four times. They stop what they're doing and look at each other.)

KAY. It could be Mom.

MICHAEL. Damn, you're right. *(answers phone)* Hello. – She's not here. Who is this anyway? – Dudley? What do you want her for? She borrowed my car to meet you at Piks. Oh – well where are you? What are you doing at Max's? Grady said y'all were going to be at Piks. Boy is she going to be mad. Okay, I'll tell her. Bye. *(hangs up phone)*

KAY. What's going on?

MICHAEL. Nickie had a date with her new boyfriend and it's all messed up.

KAY. What's Sadie Hawkins Day?

MICHAEL. Where did you hear about that?

---

*See Music Use Note on page 3

KAY. Some kids were talking about it at school. They said the girls get dressed up like Sadie Hawkins. They put freckles all over their faces and wear torn clothes and get to ask a boy out on a date. Is that true?

MICHAEL. Yeah.

KAY. What for?

MICHAEL. The Sadie Hawkins dance.

KAY. There's a dance?

MICHAEL. Of course. That's when they announce the nominations for favorites.

KAY. That sounds wonderful.

MICHAEL. I guess.

KAY. How come I never saw you dressed up like that?

MICHAEL. Because every time the dance comes around I get sick. There isn't anybody I want to ask anyway.

KAY. Nobody you want to ask? How could that be?

MICHAEL. Do you mind?

KAY. I bet that's the only way I'm ever going to get a date. Only I'm going to have to wait two more years.

MICHAEL. Maybe not.

KAY. Nobody, but nobody in the eighth grade wants to date an eleven-year old. I won't even need a brassiere until I get to the tenth grade. That is, if I'm lucky.

MICHAEL. If you really want to wear a brassiere, you can buy an A cup and put socks in them.

KAY. That's gross. Who ever heard of such a thing?

MICHAEL. That's what I did in the seventh grade.

KAY. You did not.

MICHAEL. I most certainly did.

KAY. What for?

MICHAEL. Well – to look like I had something.

KAY. Did Mom know you did that?

MICHAEL. I don't remember. Everybody was doing it.

KAY. With my luck the socks would fall out between classes. I guess I just have to wait. I'll have to wait and wait and wait!

MICHAEL. What happened to you today?

KAY. It just so happens that I may not get to play in the school band because they probably don't have a band uniform small enough to fit me. The band director said he never heard of an eleven year old in the eighth grade before. I think I'll kill myself.

MICHAEL. Can't they fix one to fit you?

KAY. I don't know. He said he would 'look into it'.

MICHAEL. So you're worrying over nothing.

KAY. The uniform is one problem. The other problem is the hat. I look stupid in it. It's only about four sizes too big.

MICHAEL. Maybe you should try out for cheerleader.

KAY. When is Sadie Hawkins day anyway?

MICHAEL. In April.

KAY. If you find somebody to ask would you let me put the freckles on your face?

MICHAEL. Sure. Why not?

KAY. How many of these problems do you want me to work?

MICHAEL. How many did you do?

KAY. Three.

MICHAEL. Three? That's fantastic. I wish you could take the test for me tomorrow.

KAY. I think I'll practice my flute.

MICHAEL. Okay. I'd better get back to barffy algebra.

KAY. You know, it would be just my luck to drop my flute on my toe. Then I'd be crippled for the rest of my life.

MICHAEL. What time is it?

KAY. Later than you think.

MICHAEL. What time is that?

KAY. *Son las cinco y media.*

MICHAEL. *Como se llama?*

KAY. *Me llama,* Kay.

MICHAEL. *Como esta usted,* Kay?

KAY. *Muy bien, gracias. Y usted?*

MICHAEL. You want me to help you with your Spanish?

KAY. What time is Mom coming home?

MICHAEL. What is today?

KAY. It's her bowling day.

MICHAEL. Any minute. Damn, why did I let Nickie borrow the car?

KAY. She probably had a wreck.

MICHAEL. Thanks a lot.

KAY. Well, didn't you tell me she wrecked her dad's car?

MICHAEL. I didn't tell you she wrecked her dad's car. I told you she had a wreck in her dad's car.

KAY. Same thing.

MICHAEL. It is not!

KAY. It is so!

MICHAEL. Is not!

KAY. Is so!

MICHAEL. Is not!

KAY. So!

MICHAEL. Not!

KAY. Who cares anyway!

MICHAEL. I do!

KAY. Well, I don't. I can't drive anyway.

MICHAEL. Well I'm sure not going to teach you.

KAY. Then Aunt Isabelle will teach me.

MICHAEL. Then you'll have to wait until you're fourteen.

KAY. Then I'll wait. Here's your dumb algebra book. *(closes book with irritation)*

MICHAEL. I'm sorry.

KAY. You are not.

MICHAEL. I am so.

KAY. You are not.

MICHAEL. Am so.

KAY. Am not.

MICHAEL. You're just mad because of the band uniform.

KAY. So what!!!

(Runs out of the room. **MICHAEL** *puts* Too Pooped To Pop* *on again.* **NICKIE** *enters.)*

NICKIE. Turn that thing off. I'm about to split a gut.

*(***MICHAEL** *turns record player off.)*

MICHAEL. Where are my keys?

NICKIE. I left them in the car.

MICHAEL. Dudley called. They went to Max's instead.

NICKIE. Now you tell me.

MICHAEL. I couldn't very well tell you if you weren't here.

NICKIE. Are they coming over?

MICHAEL. They better not be. We have to study.

NICKIE. Well what did he say?

MICHAEL. I told you. They're at Max's.

NICKIE. That's all he said?

MICHAEL. Yeah.

NICKIE. Boy that really burns me. – How many problems did you get done?

MICHAEL. Where's my hamburger?

NICKIE. You didn't really want one did you?

MICHAEL. I'm starved.

NICKIE. Tough luck. You should have come with me. *(looks at algebra problems)* You did all these?

MICHAEL. Kay did them.

NICKIE. Fantastic. How come she didn't finish them?

MICHAEL. We had a fight.

NICKIE. Couldn't you have waited until after she finished working them? You're not too bright sometimes, Goodman.

---

*See Music Use Note on page 3

MICHAEL. Thanks. Now you want to give me some help?

NICKIE. I can't work any of those stupid problems now. I'm too mad to think. And if Most Handsome doesn't call me in the next five minutes, he's not going to get my vote this year.

MICHAEL. Who would you vote for instead?

NICKIE. I don't know. There must be somebody.

MICHAEL. How about Horace Beaman?

NICKIE. Who's that?

MICHAEL. That good-looking guy in algebra class.

NICKIE. Where does he sit?

MICHAEL. Next to Lonnie Kay Rickey.

NICKIE. Him! Do you know him?

MICHAEL. Yeah, would you vote for him?

NICKIE. Who does he go with?

MICHAEL. Rosalee Cape. Well, would you vote for him or not?

NICKIE. That depends. If he got nominated, I might.

MICHAEL. Yeah, but he won't get nominated. The same people get nominated and the same people win. Every year it's the same favorites. Nobody else ever gets a chance!

NICKIE. What are you getting so freaked-out about?

MICHAEL. I'm not.

NICKIE. You are so.

MICHAEL. And the same people nominate the same people every year too!

NICKIE. Do you want to get nominated for something?

MICHAEL. I just think everybody should have a chance, that's all.

NICKIE. What do you want to get nominated for? Most beautiful?

MICHAEL. Noooooo! Never mind.

NICKIE. What? Most Likely to Succeed?

MICHAEL. You have to make straight A's to get that one. My grades aren't good enough.

NICKIE. Aren't you going to tell me?

MICHAEL. No.

NICKIE. Come on. Tell me!

MICHAEL. It doesn't matter anyway because the same people get nominated and the same people win. Just like you do for Student Council.

NICKIE. I guess it's just luck.

MICHAEL. Do you realize this has been going on since junior high school? I mean, like Grady's been voted most handsome since the eighth grade. Four years in a row. And this year we're graduating.

NICKIE. I really never thought about it. I guess you're right. But you know, like Student Council – what difference does it make? They don't do anything anyway.

MICHAEL. They do so.

NICKIE. They do not. I should know. I've been in for – this is my third year.

MICHAEL. Well they should.

NICKIE. Like what?

MICHAEL. I don't know. But they should do something.

NICKIE. Well if you can think of something, I'll suggest it.

MICHAEL. Okay, but it's not the same thing.

NICKIE. I just hope Grady asks me to go steady with him again. I can't wait to see his face when I turn him down.

MICHAEL. Why don't you just go on over to Max's.

NICKIE. And get the reputation that I run after boys? No thank you. If anyone is going to do any running, it's going to be Grady Van Vleck.

MICHAEL. Why do you want to go steady with him anyway. I mean, except for the obvious reasons.

NICKIE. Because I like to park and make-out and I've heard some fantastic stories about how he can neck.

MICHAEL. That's the reason?

NICKIE. What's wrong with that? I get horny too you know.

MICHAEL. I hate that expression.

NICKIE. Okay – I have feelings. Is that better?

MICHAEL. Much.

NICKIE. Don't you?

MICHAEL. Of course I do, but I don't have to broadcast it to the whole world.

NICKIE. Then how is anyone going to know about it?

MICHAEL. You better be careful or you're going to have to get married someday.

NICKIE. Not me. All I do is neck. When things get too hairy, I quit. Well, most of the time.

MICHAEL. Doesn't that make them mad?

NICKIE. It never made Floyd mad. I just told him that if he wanted to live with me for he rest of his life just go right ahead. Stopped him every time.

MICHAEL. You did not.

NICKIE. I did so. Ask Floyd if you don't believe me.

MICHAEL. I can't ask him that.

NICKIE. You're still teaching Sunday school aren't you?

MICHAEL. I can't believe you told him that.

NICKIE. Goody Goodman rides again. I'll give him five more minutes to call.

MICHAEL. Oh no! What are you planning?

NICKIE. I don't know yet.

(We hear the sound of **KAY** *practicing her flute.)*

What's that?

MICHAEL. Kay is trying out for the band.

NICKIE. Good luck.

MICHAEL. She's going to need it. There aren't any uniforms small enough to fit her.

NICKIE. What I don't understand is how she got to be in the eighth grade at eleven. What is she anyway, some kind of genius?

MICHAEL. She started the first grade when she was four.

NICKIE. Spare me! How did that happen?

MICHAEL. I don't know. I taught her to read and write and by the time she was four she was in the first grade.

NICKIE. Hey, I've got an idea. But you and the brain have to help me.

MICHAEL. What do we have to do?

NICKIE. Well, I can't drive to Max's by myself. You and the brain have to come with me. That way you can get that hamburger you're dying to eat.

MICHAEL. Kay doesn't like to go to Max's. She doesn't like their French fries.

NICKIE. Then she can go along for the ride. It'll look good if she's in the car.

MICHAEL. She won't go.

NICKIE. What do I have to do to get her to stop playing her flute?

MICHAEL. *(yells)* Kaaaaaay!

(The music stops.)

I want to ask you something.

KAY'S VOICE. Waaaaaat?

MICHAEL. *(yells)* You want to go for a ride?

KAY'S VOICE. Nooooooooo!

(We hear the sound of the flute again.)

NICKIE. Something went wrong.

MICHAEL. If she doesn't want to go for a ride, she sure doesn't want to go to Max's.

NICKIE. Try again.

MICHAEL. What am I supposed to say?

NICKIE. I don't know. She's your sister. Think of something she likes then ask her if she wants to do it and we'll just happen to make a stop at Max's.

MICHAEL. What a good idea.

NICKIE. What does she like?

MICHAEL. I'm thinking.

NICKIE. Hurry up. They might leave.

MICHAEL. Well – no, that would never work.

NICKIE. What? Try it! It'll work. It'll work!

MICHAEL. No, it's stupid.

NICKIE. What is it?

MICHAEL. I could ask her if she'd like to drive.

NICKIE. It's stupid.

MICHAEL. I can't think of anything else.

NICKIE. Great. So thanks to you, my love life is going down the drain.

MICHAEL. It's not my fault that she doesn't want to go.

NICKIE. I'm going to have a new category added to the favorites in the annual this year, and you're going to win it.

MICHAEL. What?

NICKIE. 'The friend that lets you down the most'!

MICHAEL. Gee, thanks.

NICKIE. I'm not kidding, Goodman. All I have to do is bring it up in Student Council.

MICHAEL. What do you want me to do? Twist her arm?

NICKIE. It'll be a cinch. Rosy Jackson is editor of the annual this year and she just happens to be president of Student Council and I've got a picture of you taken at Padre Island last summer that would be just perfect. Something I've been saving.

MICHAEL. You have not.

NICKIE. Try me!

MICHAEL. *(in horror)* KAY! COME IN HERE RIGHT NOW!!

(The music stops. **KAY** *enters.* **SHE** *is slightly hysterical in response to* **MICHAEL***'s hysteria)*

KAY. What? What happened?

MICHAEL. You want to learn to drive, right?

KAY. What?

MICHAEL. I told Nickie that you wanted to learn to drive and we decided that now would be a good time for you to have your first lesson.

KAY. What?

MICHAEL. Before Mom gets home.

KAY. You scared the hell out of me, Michael.

MICHAEL. I'm sorry. What about it?

KAY. Are you crazy? I can't even see over the steering wheel.

MICHAEL. You can use a pillow.

KAY. What pillow?

MICHAEL. Any pillow!

KAY. Why are you freaking-out at me?

MICHAEL. Because we have to hurry and do it before Mom gets home.

KAY. I don't want to learn to drive today.

MICHAEL. Please!

KAY. What's going on here?

MICHAEL. What do you mean? Nothing's going on.

KAY. Something's going on here. What is it?

MICHAEL. Nothing.

KAY. If you tell me what's going on, I might let you give me a driving lesson.

MICHAEL. *(deferring to NICKIE)* Well—

NICKIE. Look, I want to meet my boyfriend at Max's, except that I don't want it to look like I'm running after him, so I asked Michael to ask you if you wanted to go to Max's with us so I can see him without looking like a toad.

KAY. Their French fries stink.

NICKIE. I'll buy you anything you want.

KAY. Okay.

NICKIE. You mean you'll go?

KAY. Why not?

MICHAEL. Fantastic!

KAY. On one condition!

MICHAEL. What?

KAY. I drive.

MICHAEL. No.

KAY. Then I don't go.

MICHAEL. But you promised.

KAY. I did not promise.

NICKIE. Go get a pillow, Michael.

KAY. I'll get one.

(She dashes off to get the pillow.)

MICHAEL. See what you did!

NICKIE. Don't worry. You can hold on to the steering wheel.

MICHAEL. What picture at Padre island?

NICKIE. That's for me to know and you to find out! And you will if you're not very careful.

*(**KAY** enters with pillow.)*

KAY. I'm ready.

*(**MICHAEL** looks for her car keys.)*

MICHAEL. Oh god! I can't find my car keys!

NICKIE. That's because I left them in the car.

MICHAEL. Oh, right.

(The phone rings.)

KAY. Don't answer it. Let's go.

MICHAEL. *(going to phone and answering it)* It might be Mom. – Hello. – Hi, we were just coming to meet you. *(to **NICKIE**)* It's Grady.

NICKIE. Tell him I'm not here.

MICHAEL. How can I tell him you're not here when I just told him we're coming to meet him? I wish you'd make up your mind.

NICKIE. Oh, never mind. *(Takes receiver from **MICHAEL**. Speaks to Grady in a very different voice.)* Hi, good looking. I guess I missed you at Piks. ...No kidding, what happened?

KAY. Now what?

MICHAEL. I don't know. We have to wait.

KAY. Barf!

NICKIE. *(to Grady)* Spray paint? On the house or the sidewalk? Both! Who's bright idea was that?

KAY. Are we going or not?

MICHAEL. I don't know.

KAY. You're always waiting on somebody else.

MICHAEL. I am not.

KAY. You are so.

NICKIE. *(to them)* Do you mind? I can't hear. *(back to Grady)* What did you say to the police?

KAY. *(whispers)* Well, am I going to get to drive or not? Or do I have to wait and ask Nickie?

MICHAEL. Can't you let her finish her phone conversation?

NICKIE. *(to Grady)* You're lucky you didn't get arrested!

KEY. Who is she talking to?

MICHAEL. Most Handsome.

KAY. What year?

MICHAEL. Every year. He's in our class. Grady Van Vleck.

KAY. He's ugly.

MICHAEL. Be quiet.

KAY. *(whispers)* Well he is.

MICHAEL. He is not.

KAY. Is so.

NICKIE. *(to them)* Shhhhhh!

MICHAEL. Then who would you choose?

KAY. Dallas Wolf. I think he's beautiful.

MICHAEL. Who is Dallas Wolf?

KAY. Just the most beautiful boy in the eighth grade.

MICHAEL. Eight grade! What's that got to do with anything?

KAY. Everything!

NICKIE. Oh wow, when? *(to **MICHAEL**)* Grady's dad bought him a motor cycle and he's going to take me for a ride.

MICHAEL. When? Now?

NICKIE. *(back on phone)* What? Sure, now is great. Do you know where Michael lives? You did? When? Fantastic. I'll be out front. Bye. *(hangs up phone)* He's coming over to pick me up. *(to* **KAY***)* You don't have to go to Max's.

KAY. I can't believe this.

MICHAEL. How does he know where I live?

NICKIE. Remember last week when somebody toilet papered your front yard?

MICHAEL. *(excited)* Grady did that?

NICKIE. No, stupid. He and Dudley and some other guys rode over to see it, that's all.

MICHAEL. Oh.

NICKIE. You can finish the algebra problems while I'm gone.

MICHAEL. Does he have a license?

NICKIE. I don't know. God, Goodman, you're really too much. I didn't ask. If he knows how to drive it, what difference does it make?

MICHAEL. I don't know.

NICKIE. Can I borrow a scarf? I don't want my hair to get ruined.

MICHAEL. *(going for scarf)* What color?

KAY. May I go now?

MICHAEL. Where are you going?

KAY. I just wondered if you were through with me?

MICHAEL. What are you complaining about? You don't like Max's anyway.

KAY. That's not the point.

(She exits.)

MICHAEL. *(after her)* Then what is?

NICKIE. What's the matter with her?

*(***KAY*** enters.)*

KAY. And the next time you ask me if I want to do something that you have to talk me into I would appreciate it if you would have the courtesy to let me do it! Is that too much to ask, sister dear?

MICHAEL. No, it isn't too much to ask.

KAY. Don't you have to ask Nickie first?

MICHAEL. Would you mind?

KAY. Sometimes you worry me!

(She exits.)

NICKIE. God, what's with her?

MICHAEL. She's disappointed.

NICKIE. What about?

MICHAEL. We did promise to let her drive, you know.

NICKIE. I can't believe she took that seriously.

MICHAEL. What do you mean? We were getting ready to go out to the car before Grady called.

NICKIE. Well, she'll get over it.

MICHAEL. I know, but we did lead her on.

NICKIE. First you're scared to death to let her drive; now you're sorry you didn't let her. Goodman, you're weird.

MICHAEL. And you're not I suppose.

NICKIE. I expect to see those algebra problems finished by the time I get back.

MICHAEL. All of them?

NICKIE. Remember, I have a picture that you don't want anybody to see.

MICHAEL. That's not fair.

NICKIE. Tough Titty.

MICHAEL. I don't even know what the picture is.

NICKIE. So?

MICHAEL. So maybe you're making it up.

NICKIE. I could be, but I'm not. Believe me, if you value your reputation!

MICHAEL. *(with some alarm)* It's not that day I drank that pint of gin, is it?

NICKIE. Who had her trusty Brownie with her?

MICHAEL. Damn, I hate algebra.

NICKIE. Where's that scarf for my hair?

MICHAEL. *(going to drawer, taking scarf out)* I'll get it. – Is this okay?

NICKIE. Sure.

MICHAEL. When's he going to be here?

NICKIE. Any minute. I'll meet in him the front yard.

MICHAEL. Have a good time.

NICKIE. I usually do.

MICHAEL. Tell Grady hello for me.

NICKIE. You know, if you weren't such a jerk, you could go for a ride on Dudley's bike – and cheat on the test tomorrow.

MICHAEL. The last time I rode a bike I burned my leg. I don't think I want to do that again.

NICKIE. Well, I've done all I can. Have a good time.

(She exits.)

MICHAEL. You too.

(MICHAEL goes through her record collection. She finds and puts on Sixty Minute Man* *and pantomimes the words.)*

(KAY enters. She watches MICHAEL carefully.)

KAY. You're off. Way off.

(MICHAEL continues to pantomime the record with more intensity.)

You're still off.

(MICHAEL stops and takes needle off the record.)

MICHAEL. Have a heart. I just started working on this one for the senior show. And it's not until the end of the year.

KAY. Are you planning on doing that one at Young Judea too?

---

*See Music Use Note on page 3

MICHAEL. I don't know. I might? Why?

KAY. I just wondered.

MICHAEL. What's wrong with doing it at Young Judea?

KAY. I didn't say anything was wrong with doing it. But you'll have to work on it a lot more.

MICHAEL. I know that. I told you I just started working on it.

KAY. Is your friend gone yet?

MICHAEL. She's your friend too.

KAY. She is not. I don't even know her first name.

MICHAEL. You do so. Her name is Susan.

KAY. Then why do you call her Nickie?

MICHAEL. Because that's her last name. Everybody calls her that.

KAY. She calls you Goodman.

MICHAEL. Well, it's my name, isn't it?

KAY. No! Your name is Michael Lee Goodman. I don't see why she has to call you Goodman. I sure wouldn't want anybody to call me Goodman.

MICHAEL. Well I'm not you.

KAY. She ought to call you Michael. It sounds weird for a girl to be called by her last name.

MICHAEL. Not to me.

KAY. Well, you're weird.

MICHAEL. Thanks for the compliment.

KAY. Why did you have to do that?

MICHAEL. I'm sorry. I really thought we were going for a drive.

KAY. Yeah, but you're always doing something like that.

MICHAEL. Like what?

KAY. You say you're going to do something and then you don't do it because some friend of yours doesn't want to or something like that.

MICHAEL. That's not true.

KAY. It is too.

MICHAEL. Like what for instance? Give me an example.

KAY. I can't think of anything right now, but I will.

MICHAEL. I don't know what you're talking about.

KAY. Like the day you said you were going to take me and my friend, Greta, horseback riding, and some friend of yours called and instead you went roller-skating with them.

MICHAEL. I took you with me didn't I?

KAY. Yeah, but I wanted to go horseback riding, and you didn't even ask if I wanted to go skating. You just told me that we were going.

MICHAEL. Why didn't you say something?

KAY. I did, but you wouldn't listen to me. I tried.

MICHAEL. I don't remember.

KAY. And what about Greta? She didn't get to go anywhere because she absolutely hates to roller skate.

MICHAEL. I take you a lot of places.

KAY. I know.

MICHAEL. I even take you places when I don't have to.

KAY. I know. But you sure do change your mind a lot when it comes to your friends.

MICHAEL. I like to do things with my friends. What's wrong with that all of a sudden? You're beginning to sound like Mom.

KAY. I am not!

MICHAEL. You are so. She's always telling me that I do too much for my friends. How can you do too much for your friends? Isn't that what friends are for? To do things for?

KAY. I don't know. How do I know? I only have one friend and she has asthma most of the time.

MICHAEL. Well, you do things for her, don't you?

KAY. Yeah, but not when I'm supposed to be doing something with you.

MICHAEL. I guess I'm supposed to give up all my friends?

KAY. Oh, never mind.

MICHAEL. Is that what I'm supposed to do?

KAY. Forget I ever brought it up, okay?

MICHAEL. I'll be glad to.

KAY. You want to practice your new record?

MICHAEL. You want to help me?

KAY. Sure.

MICHAEL. Great. If I get it worked up, I might do it at Young Judea.

(She puts Sixty Minute Man* *on and pantomimes as* **KAY** *watches and nods approvingly.)*

*(***NICKIE*** enters.)*

What are you doing back here so soon? What happened to Grady?

NICKIE. You have to come with us.

MICHAEL. Why?

NICKIE. Dudley doesn't want to ride his bike without having a girl on the back if Grady has a girl on the back of his.

MICHAEL. What's that got to do with me?

NICKIE. You're the girl who's going to ride on the back of Dudley's bike.

MICHAEL. Not me.

KAY. I'll go.

NICKIE. That's okay. Come on, Michael. I promised him you would. So come on.

MICHAEL. I hardly know Dudley.

NICKIE. So? He hardly knows you. I'll introduce you.

MICHAEL. You've been out there all that time?

NICKIE. Dudley is very stubborn.

MICHAEL. I don't know.

NICKIE. Look, I'm not supposed to tell you this, but he thinks you're cute and he's been wanting to meet you

---

*See Music Use Note on page 3

since the Halloween Dance when you did that pantomime to that Spike Jones record.

MICHAEL. I was terrible that night.

NICKIE. Dudley thought you were great!

MICHAEL. Okay, let me get a scarf.

NICKIE. I knew I could count on you. You're really the best.

MICHAEL. *(to KAY)* Tell Mom I'll be right back.

NICKIE. Hey, that's the one!

KAY. Okay.

MICHAEL. I hope I don't burn my leg again.

NICKIE. Best All 'Round. That's the one, right?

MICHAEL. What's the one?

NICKIE. Of course, I should have known.

MICHAEL. Do you mind? I find this very embarrassing.

NICKIE. I'll see what I can do.

MICHAEL. What do you mean?

NICKIE. Rosy is also on the nominating committee for class favorites too.

KAY. Who's Rosy?

NICKIE. She's a toad.

KAY. Oh.

MICHAEL. What can you do? What? Tell me.

NICKIE. Just bring your name up, that's all. Just bring your name up.

MICHAEL. I didn't know you could do that.

NICKIE. There's a lot of things you don't know, Goodman. Now, can we go now?

MICHAEL. What about the algebra problems?

KAY. I'll do them.

MICHAEL. You will? That's fantastic. You're fantastic. You're wonderful.

KAY. Barf!

MICHAEL. I really mean it.

KAY. I'm just bored.

MICHAEL. Stay that way – only until you finish the problems of course.

NICKIE. Hurry up, Goodman, before Grady gets away again.

(She exits.)

MICHAEL. Remember, I'll only be gone about twenty minutes.

KAY. Don't burn your leg.

MICHAEL. See you later.

(She exits.)

KAY. *(yelling off to* **MICHAEL**) See what I mean! *(She picks up the algebra book, opens it randomly and reads.)* 'A man rows 12 miles upstream in 4 hours. He rows 20 miles downstream in 2 hours and 30 minutes. Find the man's rate of rowing in still water and the speed of the current.' — Oh, who the hell cares!

(Slams book closed. Goes over to record player, puts on Too Pooped to Pop* *and pantomimes to it.)*

END OF ACT ONE

---

*See Music Use Note on page 3

ACT TWO

(Michael's bedroom. She is dressed in her Sadie Hawkins outfit: White sneakers, white socks, a short raggedy skirt, a blouse made of red bandanna material. Her hair is braided into two limp pigtails. SHE is at the mirror putting on bright red lipstick.)

MICHAEL. *(yells)* Kaaaaay! I'm ready for the freckles.

(KAY enters dressed in her band uniform. SHE carries her flute in its case.)

KAY. *(exasperated)* Coming. Where is it?

MICHAEL. On the bed with the rest of the stuff.

(KAY crosses to bed, puts her flute case down, finds eyebrow pencil, takes top off.)

KAY. Where's your pencil sharpener?

MICHAEL. In my desk. Why?

KAY. This eyebrow pencil's dull.

MICHAEL. It's supposed to be that way.

KAY. Not *this* dull. *(shows it to MICHAEL)*

MICHAEL. Okay.

(KAY goes to desk, finds pencil sharpener and sharpens pencil while MICHAEL puts on her rouge.)

MICHAEL. Not too sharp, okay?

KAY. Okay.

MICHAEL. How do I look?

KAY. You need your freckles. Okay now. How many do you want?

MICHAEL. I don't know. Just enough to make it look good.

KAY. Okay.

(She applies large freckles.)

MICHAEL. What are you doing?

KAY. What do you mean, what am I doing? I'm putting on your freckles.

MICHAEL. Not too big, okay?

KAY. I know what I'm doing, Michael.

MICHAEL. I just don't want them too big.

KAY. Okay.

MICHAEL. The pencil's too sharp.

KAY. It has to be sharp.

MICHAEL. Well then, be more careful, it hurts.

KAY. I'm almost through.

MICHAEL. Put one on my nose.

KAY. Okay.

MICHAEL. This is really stupid.

KAY. I know.

MICHAEL. Why did I let Nickie talk me into going to this dumb dance?

KAY. I know why. To hear your nomination for Best All 'Round.

MICHAEL. Nobody said I was going to be nominated. Nickie said she would mention my name. That's not exactly being nominated. – Put another one on my nose. One looks stupid.

KAY. You want some on your arms too?

MICHAEL. No! Barf.

KAY. What's the matter with freckles on your arms? Greta has freckles on her arms.

MICHAEL. Greta *has* freckles.

KAY. I know. That's what I'm trying to tell you.

MICHAEL. I don't need them on my arms.

KAY. You most certainly do if you want to be authentic.

MICHAEL. Are you through?

KAY. Have it your way. *(hands MICHAEL the eyebrow pencil)* I was only trying to help.

MICHAEL. What time do you have to be there?

KAY. I can't help it if I'm going to be at your dumb old dance. I'm in the Baker Junior High Dance Band. It's not my fault we're plying for your dumb Sadie Hawkins Dance.

MICHAEL. What time?

KAY. I have to be there at seven on the dot, and we start playing around eight.

MICHAEL. Fine.

KAY. What was I supposed to do? Tell Mr. Elliot that I couldn't play my flute tonight because my sister is going to be at the dance and doesn't want me there.

MICHAEL. You could have pretended you were sick or something.

KAY. With what?

MICHAEL. I don't know. Chicken Pox.

KAY. For one night?

MICHAEL. Oh never mind. *(She goes back to her mirror and sees the huge freckles.)* WHAT HAPPENED?

KAY. *(scared from MICHAEL's hysteria)* What happened?

MICHAEL. What is this supposed to be? *(refers to freckles)*

KAY. What do you mean?

MICHAEL. What do you mean, what do I mean? What is all this?

KAY. Freckles of course!

MICHAEL. Blotches. You put blotches all over my face. Now I have to wash it off and start all over again.

KAY. They're freckles.

MICHAEL. They are not.

KAY. Instead of a thank you, I'm getting screamed at.

MICHAEL. I told you, not too big.

KAY. Next time, do them yourself.

MICHAEL. I will. *(She puts cold cream on her face.)*

KAY. Blame it on Nickie why don't you. She's the one who talked you into going to the dance.

MICHAEL. Oh, shut up!

KAY. I wish Mom were here.

MICHAEL. Would you mind waiting in the other room?

KAY. I'm sorry.

MICHAEL. I told you not to make them too big, and you went ahead and did it.

KAY. I like big freckles. – When's Nickie getting here?

MICHAEL. What time is it?

KAY. Son las seis y quince!

MICHAEL. I'm not in the mood.

KAY. Fifteen after six and I have to be there at seven on the dot.

MICHAEL. I heard you before.

KAY. I can't be late, Michael.

MICHAEL. You're not going to be late. Nickie said she would be here at six-thirty the latest.

KAY. Where do you meet your date?

MICHAEL. None of your business.

KAY. Are you going to be mad all night?

MICHAEL. No, just part of the night.

KAY. I said I was sorry.

MICHAEL. I'm meeting him at the dance.

KAY. How come you're not picking him up at his house, like the boys do the girls?

MICHAEL. I don't know. Nickie said we could meet them at the dance. What difference does it make?

KAY. Because it's not a real date.

MICHAEL. It is so a real date.

KAY. No, it isn't. If you're not picking him up at this house and meeting his parents and his brothers and sisters, then it's not a real date.

MICHAEL. Then what is it?

KAY. I don't know. You're just meeting him there.

MICHAEL. Spare me, okay?

KAY. Okay! *(pause)* Did she start her period yet?

MICHAEL. *(cautious)* What are you talking about?

KAY. You know who.

MICHAEL. I do not.

KAY. You most certainly do.

MICHAEL. Who?

KAY. You know!!

MICHAEL. I don't know what you're talking about.

KAY. Nickie!

MICHAEL. How did you find out about that?

KAY. I heard two people talking about it yesterday, and last week too.

MICHAEL. You're kidding. Where were you?

KAY. Trying to go to sleep.

MICHAEL. You were eavesdropping.

KAY. I was not.

MICHAEL. You better not tell anybody.

KAY. What do you take me for?

MICHAEL. You're not supposed to know. Nobody is.

KAY. Then you shouldn't be discussing it in loud voices at eleven o'clock at night when you think I'm asleep.

MICHAEL. You were supposed to be.

KAY. But I wasn't.

MICHAEL. Don't say anything in front of Nickie. She's upset enough.

KAY. What's going to happen if she doesn't – start?

MICHAEL. Grady's trying to find out the name of a doctor that one of the cheerleaders went to last year.

KAY. One of the cheerleaders? Which one?

MICHAEL. I'm not going to tell you which one.

KAY. Why not?

MICHAEL. Because I'm not. It's none of your business.

KAY. Who cares anyway?

MICHAEL. Just forget about it, okay?

KAY. Your freckles are too small.

MICHAEL. They're *my* freckles.

KAY. Where's Nickie?

MICHAEL. Call her house and find out if you're so worried.

KAY. What's her number? I will.

MICHAEL. You will not.

KAY. You just said to call.

MICHAEL. She'll be here, okay! You're not going to be late!!

KAY. Aren't you finished yet?

MICHAEL. Finally.

KAY. Why are you going if you don't want to go?

MICHAEL. I told you. Nickie talked me into going.

KAY. Why?

MICHAEL. I don't know. I guess she wanted to double.

KAY. That's the reason you're going?

MICHAEL. One of the reasons.

KAY. What's the other one?

MICHAEL. I can't tell you. It's a secret.

KAY. I won't tell.

MICHAEL. Promise?

KAY. Cross my hear, hope to die, stick a needle in my eye.

MICHAEL. Nickie said I might get nominated. You know. For a favorite.

KAY. I know that! I want to hear you say it.

MICHAEL. I can't. Besides – nobody is supposed to know.

KAY. You know. I know.

MICHAEL. That's because Nickie is on the nominating committee. God, I hope I don't get it. I would just die.

KAY. Say it out loud.

MICHAEL. I can't. You say it.

KAY. Well, not most beautiful, or most likely to succeed, or most popular; so what's left?

MICHAEL. I don't know. What's left?

KAY. Let's see, ohhhhhhhhh, I know! Best All 'Round. Could that be it?

MICHAEL. I guess so.

KAY. It's the only one left. My sister, Best All 'Round.

MICHAEL. Don't get your hopes up, because I probably won't get it, because the same people get it every year. – And don't say a word to anybody!

KAY. Did I say anything to anybody about Nickie missing her period?

MICHAEL. Could you please stop talking about that! You're going to get me into trouble.

KAY. Who cares anyway?

MICHAEL. She could get expelled from school for one, and then she couldn't graduate.

KAY. I didn't think of that.

MICHAEL. And then there's her parents. They would kill her.

KAY. Why don't they just get married?

MICHAEL. They don't want to get married! Grady has a scholarship to go to LSU and Nickie is going to Beauty School as soon as she graduates. What's she going to do with a baby?

KAY. Freak-out time.

MICHAEL. Well, you ask a stupid question!

KAY. I guess she should have been more careful.

MICHAEL. I guess she should have.

KAY. Why aren't you entertaining tonight?

MICHAEL. I don't entertain at all the dances you know.

KAY. Most of them.

MICHAEL. I wasn't asked. They're not doing that kind of thing for this one.

KAY. Could you drive me over and then come back. I'm getting worried.

MICHAEL. If she's not here in five minutes, I will. Okay?

KAY. Okay.

MICHAEL. I'm sorry I yelled at you.

KAY. That's all right.

MICHAEL. No, it isn't. I couldn't help myself, but I'm sorry anyway.

KAY. I'm not mad at you, you know.

MICHAEL. Just don't say anything else, okay?

KAY. My lips are sealed and mum is the word and your secret will die with me!

MICHAEL. Good.

KAY. What time are the announcements being made?

MICHAEL. At the end of the dance.

KAY. It must be depressing for the people who don't get it.

MICHAEL. Not really. Like I said, the same people get nominated every year, so it shouldn't be a surprise for the people who lose.

KAY. Except this year, you're going to be nominated.

MICHAEL. I'm not going to be nominated, so could we please stop talking about it.

KAY. Miracles do happen you know.

MICHAEL. That's exactly what it would be. Now would you please? I'm getting a headache.

KAY. Can I say one more thing, then I won't say anything else.

MICHAEL. What?

KAY. I'd vote for you.

MICHAEL. You would?

(NICKIE bursts into the room, freaked-out and very noisy. She is dressed in her "Sadie Hawkins Outfit.")

NICKIE. You won't believe what I'm about to tell you. I can't believe it myself. Do you have any idea what Grady Van Vleck did today? You are not going to believe this. You know what he did? He and five other guys on the football team joined the army today.

MICHAEL. Dudley too?

NICKIE. Dudley got stuck taking a make-up test. Do you believe it?

MICHAEL. How did you find out?

NICKIE. Judy Gwartney called to lord it over me.

MICHAEL. Judy Gwartney. That's too much.

NICKIE. Just because she used to go with him, she thinks she has some pull.

MICHAEL. What did you say to her?

NICKIE. I told her that I already knew.

MICHAEL. You did?

NICKIE. Nooooo! But I wasn't going to let her know that. Do you believe it? He's just leaving. He'd rather go to Korea than to college. Boy, that really burns me.

MICHAEL. What are you going to do?

NICKIE. I'm going to the dance. That's what I'm going to do.

MICHAEL. Without your date?

NICKIE. You're not exactly in love with Dudley, are you?

MICHAEL. No, why?

NICKIE. Then he's got two dates! Anything wrong with that?

MICHAEL. I guess not.

KAY. Shouldn't we be going?

NICKIE. Where is *she* going?

KAY. She is part of the dance band tonight.

NICKIE. You're kidding.

MICHAEL. Nope. Baker Junior High Dance Band.

NICKIE. I can't wait to see Grady's face when we both show up with Dudley.

MICHAEL. You mean he's going to *be* there.

NICKIE. Of course he's going to be there. He doesn't have to report until next week. Judy Gwartney told me that too. Plus she gave me the name of a doctor for you know what, do you believe it?

MICHAEL. No.

NICKIE. I can't repeat what I said to her in front of children. – Great freckles.

KAY. *(picking up her flute)* Let's go.

MICHAEL. *(to NICKIE)* Thanks. *(to KAY)* See.

NICKIE. They look real.

MICHAEL. What about the nominations? Did you talk to you know who?

NICKIE. I did everything I could without seeming obvious.

MICHAEL. What do you think?

NICKIE. I think you should stop talking about this to me or anyone else, and especially not in front of anybody.

KAY. It's okay; I know everything. I'll meet you in the car. *(She exits.)*

NICKIE. What does she mean, 'she knows everything'?

MICHAEL. *(getting her purse)* Nothing.

NICKIE. It sounded like something.

MICHAEL. She does that all the time.

NICKIE. I'm beginning to wonder if she knows the name of a doctor.

MICHAEL. Gosh, I hope you start tonight.

NICKIE. Believe me, if I do, I'll make sure everybody knows. In the meantime, let's go find father-to-be and congratulate him on becoming a soldier. Maybe I'll stick a grenade up his you know what.

MICHAEL. Nickie, that's awful.

NICKIE. Actually, I've got a better idea.

MICHAEL. What?

NICKIE. I could go down to the recruiting office and tell 'em he wears pink underwear.

MICHAEL. I don't get it.

NICKIE. You wouldn't. Let's go.

(lights change)

(The High School Gym. NICKIE is behind the refreshment stand tending to the punch. MICHAEL and KAY stand nearby. We hear recorded music: Cry, Crying In The Chapel, PS, I Love You, *and* Hearts Made of Stone.*)*

NICKIE. When I told Mrs. G I'd dip the punch for her, I didn't mean for the rest of the night. Where is she anyway?

MICHAEL. I think I see her over there talking to Mr. Birdwell.

NICKIE. Damn.

MICHAEL. She's looking over here. Maybe she's getting a guilty conscience. – No, I guess not. She's waving.

(MICHAEL waves back.)

KAY. I'm tired.

MICHAEL. The dance'll be over in twenty minutes.

NICKIE. I'm going to dip Mrs. G in this punch if she doesn't get over here.

KAY. I don't know if I can last twenty more minutes.

MICHAEL. What would you do if you were playing your flute right now?

KAY. I'd be playing my flute.

MICHAEL. Well, if three of your band members weren't' sneaking off and drinking bourbon, that's exactly what you'd be doing.

KAY. So?

MICHAEL. So?

KAY. Waiting around is more tiring.

MICHAEL. Well, I'm not going anywhere until the announcement for favorites are made.

KAY. What happened to Dudley?

MICHAEL. I don't know. About an hour ago he said he was getting sick and he was going out to his car. I guess he's still there.

---

*See Music Use Note on Page 3

KAY. You didn't even get to dance.

MICHAEL. I danced twice.

NICKIE. Well, would one of you mind dancing over to Mrs. G and remind her that refreshment duty is hers, not mine and I would like to be relieved.

MICHAEL. I'll go.

NICKIE. And don't come back without her.

MICHAEL. I'll try.

(She exits.)

NICKIE. Damn.

KAY. Anyway, the dance is almost over, so even if she doesn't come back, you're almost through anyway.

NICKIE. How do you like the eighth grade?

KAY. I hate it.

NICKIE. Wait 'til you get to be a senior.

KAY. Oh, I'm going to love being a senior.

NICKIE. Good luck.

KAY. How are you feeling?

NICKIE. Fine. – Why?

KAY. You know.

NICKIE. Know what?

KAY. Oh, never mind. Isn't that music romantic?

NICKIE. You're as nutty as your sister.

KAY. Don't say anything about my sister.

NICKIE. Well, pardon me for living. She happens to be my best friend, you know.

KAY. So? That doesn't give you the right to call her a nut!

NICKIE. Look, I'm not in a very good mood tonight, so don't add to it, okay?

KAY. Did you get to tell Grady off?

NICKIE. No. Grady went out to the lake with his parents.

KAY. Before he goes to boot camp.

NICKIE. You sure get around, don't you?

KAY. Everybody knows about boot camp. Who doesn't?

NICKIE. Can you see Michael? What's she doing?

KAY. I don't see her.

NICKIE. Well, can you see Mrs. G?

KAY. If you tell me what she looks like, I'll tell you if I see her.

NICKIE. She looks like a teacher.

KAY. I see two people who look like teachers. One is a man, and one is a woman.

NICKIE. Does the woman have gray hair?

KAY. Yep.

NICKIE. Is she wearing glasses and waving her hands all over the place?

KAY. Yep.

NICKIE. Do you see Michael over there?

KAY. Nope.

NICKIE. Well, where the hell is she?

KAY. Do you want me to go find her?

NICKIE. No. You better stay here. The announcements for the favorites are going to be made any minute – and it gets pretty hairy out there.

KAY. Do you think Michael is going to win the nomination?

NICKIE. The same people win every year.

KAY. Yeah, but I thought you were going to put in a good word for her.

NICKIE. A good word will hardly get a person nominated.

KAY. But she's counting on it.

NICKIE. Well, she shouldn't be. She should know better.

KAY. Yeah, but you said.

NICKIE. I said, I would mention her name. That's all I said.

KAY. Oh.

NICKIE. I'm not the only person on the committee. There are fifteen people on the committee. And they all know Michael. So she has as good a chance as anybody.

KAY. Which means, no chance at all.

NICKIE. Listen, don't worry about it. She knows it. – Damn, I knew I was going to get stuck here.

KAY. I don't feel well. It's too hot in here.

NICKIE. Why don't you take off your jacket?

KAY. I can't. I didn't wear anything under it. I forgot.

NICKIE. Just pretend you're at the beach. Nobody will notice.

KAY. You're crazy.

NICKIE. You want some punch?

KAY. It's yucky.

NICKIE. It's not my fault we ran out of ice. – I wish your sister would get her heinie back here.

KAY. I think I'm getting sick.

NICKIE. Well if you're going to throw-up, don't do it here.

KAY. Who said anything about throwing up?

*(**MICHAEL** enters.)*

NICKIE. Well, it's about time.

MICHAEL. I had to stop off in the girls' room.

NICKIE. Well, is she coming back or not?

MICHAEL. You won't believe this. But she said that a member of the Student Council like you is an example to the entire student body for thoughtfulness, and something else. She said thank you for letting her get off her feet.

NICKIE. What?

MICHAEL. That's what she said.

NICKIE. Okay, that means you have to take over for me. I have to talk to Rosy before the announcements are made. If I don't get back over here, I'll see you in the parking lot.

MICHAEL. Okay.

*(**MICHAEL** tends the refreshment stand and **NICKIE** exits.)*

NICKIE. Don't get drunk!

(**MICHAEL** *bursts out laughing.*)

KAY. What's so funny?

MICHAEL. You wouldn't understand.

KAY. Try me.

MICHAEL. It's a senior joke.

KAY. Oh.

(*The music stops abruptly. We hear the sound of a loud speaker.*)

MICHAEL. I think they're getting ready for the announcement.

KAY. I hope you don't win because it'll just go to your head–

ROSY'S VOICE. Testing one, two three. Testing. Can y'all hear me?

KAY. – and you'll get snobby and obnoxious like all the rest of the favorites, and I won't want you for my sister.

MICHAEL. Shh! Be quiet!

ROSY'S VOICE. Well, this is the moment we've all been waiting for. So all you Sadie Hawkins grab a hold of your Clem Kadiddle Hoppers and – just a minute, y'all. –

MICHAEL. They're not all snobby and obnoxious. You don't know what you're talking about.

ROSY'S VOICE. Mr. Birdwell just informed me that I didn't introduce myself. Not that I need to, but I'm Rosy Jackson and I'm President of your Student Council. Don't all clap at once. No, really–

KAY. I most certainly do.

MICHAEL. Do you mind? I'm trying to listen.

ROSY'S VOICE. I was asked by a member of the Council to inform the student body that a lot of new names were seriously considered for nominations this year.

KAY. Just remember what you said before. The same people get it every year.

ROSY'S VOICE. And that's the truth. We had a lot of new names.

KAY. And you also said that you knew you weren't going to get it.

MICHAEL. I know what I said.

ROSY'S VOICE. Well, as usual, we took a closed ballot vote and here are the nominations for this year's senior favorites.

MICHAEL. I'm dying.

KAY. So am I.

ROSY'S VOICE. First, nominated for Best All 'Round in the male category is – you guessed it – David Shields. Congratulations, David. And running against him for the third consecutive year will be Tommy Ashworth. Out of sight. And now for the nominations in the female category.

MICHAEL. Oh god.

ROSY'S VOICE. I want everybody to know that this category gave the committee a lot of trouble this year, because last year's winner, Elizabeth Crocker moved to Tennessee, so that kind of left a slot open. We considered a lot of new names for this category, before I give you the new name, I'll give you the old name first.

MICHAEL. I can't breathe.

KAY. Neither can I.

ROSY'S VOICE. Patricia Cunningham. She's not here tonight because she attending a cousin's wedding in Dallas, but she'll be back on Monday to receive her congratulations from all of you. Now – get ready everybody – the second nomination for Best All 'Round is no stranger to anyone here. And she happens to be one of my very best friends. Are you ready –

MICHAEL. Who's she talking about?

ROSY'S VOICE. Susan Nickie. Congratulations, Nickie and best of luck to all nominees for Best All 'Round. Now for the category –

(**ROSY'S VOICE** *fades into the background as* **MICHAEL** *and* **KAY** *stands there, stunned.*)

KAY. Gee. – You want to go home now? – Michael? – Yoo-hoo, Michael are you there? – Michael?

MICHAEL. I can't believe it.

KAY. Nickie said there were fifteen people on the committee and that they all knew you, so you had as good a chance as anybody.

MICHAEL. Let's go.

KAY. Don't you want to wait for Nickie? After all, she is your best friend.

MICHAEL. I said let's go!

KAY. Maybe you should find out what happened first, before you get mad.

MICHAEL. Where's your flute?

KAY. On the bandstand.

MICHAEL. Well go and get it.

KAY. I can't. The announcements are being made.

MICHAEL. Well why did you leave it on the bandstand anyway?

KAY. Because that's where you leave a flute if you're in the band.

MICHAEL. Now we'll *have* to wait.

KAY. I'm sorry.

MICHAEL. Damn! I want to go home. *(She cries.)*

KAY. Come on, Michael. I think you're wonderful. – Come on – don't cry. You don't have anything to cry about. Just because you didn't win some old stupid contest.

MICHAEL. It's not some old stupid contest.

KAY. It is so.

MICHAEL. Could you please just leave me alone?

KAY. All over some dumb old contest.

MICHAEL. It just so happens that this could have been the most important moment in my entire life, and it was ruined by a person who is supposed to be my best friend.

KAY. What I don't understand is, if you knew you weren't going to win, why are you getting so upset about it? Could you please explain that to me?

MICHAEL. Because somebody who's supposed to be my best friend turns out to be a dirty rotten turncoat.

KAY. What do you care what people think about you anyway?

MICHAEL. I care.

KAY. I like you.

MICHAEL. Of course you like me, you're my sister. You don't have any choice.

KAY. Greta doesn't like her sister.

MICHAEL. So?

KAY. So!

MICHAEL. So what!

KAY. So sister dear, it means I don't have to like you just because you're my sister. If Greta's sister was my sister I wouldn't like her either, so I wouldn't like you because you would be my sister that I wouldn't like.

MICHAEL. What?

KAY. Look, Nickie said you had as good a chance as anybody. So that must mean that they all like you too, right?

MICHAEL. How am I supposed to know?

KAY. Well?

MICHAEL. Well?

KAY. I don't know. – Too bad you weren't sick this year too.

MICHAEL. What's being sick got to do with anything?

KAY. You said you didn't come to this dumb dance before because you were sick.

MICHAEL. I wasn't sick. I never wanted to come because I knew something like this would happen.

KAY. Something like what?

MICHAEL. Are you dumb or something? Something like this!!

KAY. Oh, I give up.

ROSY'S VOICE. Well that wraps it up for this year. Best of luck to all the nominees and everybody grab your partners for the last dance.

(*We hear* Goodnight, Sweetheart.*)

KAY. I wonder who won Most Handsome?

MICHAEL. Oh, who cares. Go get your flute.

KAY. Be right back. (*exiting*)

MICHAEL. Hurry up. I want to get out of here.

KAY. Okay.

(*She is off.* **MICHAEL** *sees* **NICKIE** *coming toward her.*)

MICHAEL. Here comes the turncoat.

NICKIE. (*excited*) Wait 'til you hear the good news. It's just too good to be true. All my troubles are over.

MICHAEL. Do you know who you're talking to?

NICKIE. Of course I know who I'm talking to. My very best friend who sticks with me through thick and thin. My God, I think that rhymed. I'm a poet. Maybe I'll go to New York and write poems for a living, after I go to Beauty School of course.

MICHAEL. I hope you're having a good time.

NICKIE. Are you ready for the good news?

MICHAEL. The entire senior class knows your good new.

NICKIE. (*horrified*) You're kidding! How did they find out?

MICHAEL. Because one of your very best friends told them.

NICKIE. Who?

MICHAEL. Rosy Jackson.

NICKIE. That toad! She doesn't know.

MICHAEL. Everybody knows!!

NICKIE. What's wrong with you?

MICHAEL. Stop pretending. It's bad enough as it is.

NICKIE. What's bad enough? What are you talking about?

---

*Please See Music use Note on Page 3

MICHAEL. You're good news about Best All 'Round.

NICKIE. What good news about Best All 'Round. My news isn't about Best All 'Round. I didn't even hear the announcements. I've been out in the parking lot with somebody who shall remain nameless for the time being. Who won?

MICHAEL. You mean, you're really not talking about Best All 'Round?

NICKIE. No. I'm talking about my period. I started my period. Do you realize what that means? It means I'm not pregnant. I guess I never was. I don't have to worry anymore.

MICHAEL. That's your news?

NICKIE. What did you think I was talking about?

MICHAEL. I'm all confused.

NICKIE. I'm not pregnant anymore. I never was. What's so confusing about that?

MICHAEL. Wow.

NICKIE. Now, tell me who won what?

MICHAEL. I don't know who won – I tuned out after Rosy announced Best All 'Round.

NICKIE. You knew the odds of winning were against you. You know those dummies always vote for the same people.

MICHAEL. Not this year.

NICKIE. You're kidding.

MICHAEL. You mean you don't know that you got the nomination?

NICKIE. For what?

MICHAEL. For Best All 'Round.

NICKIE. I did not.

MICHAEL. You did so.

NICKIE. I did not.

MICHAEL. You did. It's between you and Patricia Cunningham.

NICKIE. Please say you're kidding.

MICHAEL. I thought you knew all along.

NICKIE. How could I know? The vote is secret. Mr. Birdwell counts them after the committee adjourns. I voted for you, you jerk.

MICHAEL. You did?

NICKIE. Of course I did. What do you take me for?

MICHAEL. Then you really didn't know, did you?

NICKIE. God, Goodman, how many times do I have to say so.

MICHAEL. Congratulations.

NICKIE. Me? Why me?

MICHAEL. Well, it had to be somebody.

(KAY *enters.*)

NICKIE. Yeah, but why me? It should have been you. I mean, you're the one who wants everybody to like them. I could care less.

KAY. Excuse me. I'll meet you in the car, Michael.

NICKIE. Wait a minute, brainy. We're going out to celebrate. Don't you want to come with us?

KAY. You mean you're not mad at each other. That's good news.

NICKIE. You want to hear some more good news? I started my period tonight.

KAY. I probably won't start mine for two more years.

NICKIE. If you're lucky.

MICHAEL. Nickie, she's only eleven.

KAY. Oh, right. I get it.

NICKIE. You do?

MICHAEL. Don't listen to her. She always says things like that. Don't you, Kay dear?

KAY. Always.

NICKIE. How about if I meet you both over at Max's.

KAY. Yuck.

MICHAEL. Does that mean you don't want to go?

KAY. Why can't we go to Piks?

NICKIE. Because I want to go to Max's.

KAY. Then I want to go home. Thanks for the celebration, sister, dear.

NICKIE. Look, she's your sister. I've gotta go. See you over there.

MICHAEL. Wait a minute. Who were you out in the parking lot with?

NICKIE. Floyd!

MICHAEL. *(screams with delight)* Floyd! You've got to be kidding.

NICKIE. Would I kid you about a thing like that? *(She exits.)*

KAY. Okay, who's Floyd?

MICHAEL. Her old boyfriend.

KAY. She sure does get around, doesn't she?

MICHAEL. Well, are you coming or not?

KAY. Not if you're going to Max's.

MICHAEL. Why don't you order onion rings instead of fries?

KAY. Because I hate onion rings. Barf on onion rings. Why can't we go to Piks?

MICHAEL. Because Nickie wants to go to Max's.

KAY. How come nobody ever asks me where I want to go?

MICHAEL. Nobody asked me, and I'm not complaining.

KAY. Why would anybody ask you? You don't care.

MICHAEL. I do so.

KAY. You do not.

MICHAEL. Okay, I'll take you home.

KAY. See! You're doing it again, and again and again. Never what I want. Always what she wants.

MICHAEL. How about what I want? How about that. How come nobody's ever interested in what I want?

KAY. Because you never say so.

MICHAEL. Well I'm saying so now!

KAY. What are you getting so freaked-out about?

MICHAEL. It just so happens that I do care about where we go. I care about a lot of things that I never talk about.

KAY. That's the same thing as not caring.

MICHAEL. It is not. Just because I don't say anything?

KAY. If you don't say anything, how is anybody supposed to know?

MICHAEL. Well they should!

KAY. How?

MICHAEL. It should be obvious!

KAY. That doesn't make any sense at all. How can it be obvious, if you never say anything? You think everyone is supposed to read your mind?

MICHAEL. Who said anything about reading my mind?

KAY. Do you go around reading other people's minds?

MICHAEL. Of course not.

KAY. Then don't you think it's kind of stupid for you to expect other people to be able to read yours?

MICHAEL. That's not what I said!

KAY. That is what you said!

MICHAEL. Well, it's not what I meant!

KAY. Then why don't you say what you mean?

MICHAEL. I'm trying, but you're mixing me up.

KAY. You're already mixed-up. You sure don't need any help from me.

MICHAEL. Are you through now?

KAY. I guess so. Now, do you mind, I would like to go home.

MICHAEL. And you have the nerve to criticize me.

KAY. It just so happens that I want to go home because I don't like being around you when you're in that mood.

MICHAEL. What mood?

KAY. Miss Holier than thou!!

MICHAEL. Thanks loads.

KAY. Barf!

(pause)

MICHAEL. I'm sorry. – Feel better?

KAY. That depends. What are you sorry about?

MICHAEL. I don't read other people's minds, and I should expect them to read mine. Okay?

KAY. And –

MICHAEL. And what?

KAY. And –

MICHAEL. What? What?

(KAY waits.)

Okay, I'm not holier than thou.

KAY. Great. Now where are we going?

MICHAEL. I don't know. I'll know when I get there, okay?

KAY. You're weird. – Gee. I hope Dallas Wolf stays as good-looking for the next two years so I can ask him to the Sadie Hawkins Dance.

MICHAEL. In two years you'll probably want to ask somebody else.

KAY. Not me. I'm not like your friend, Nickie.

MICHAEL. Watch what you say about Nickie. She happens to be my very best friend.

KAY. Yeah, and when she gets to be Best All 'Round, you'll be in the in-group. The real in-group.

MICHAEL. Got your flute?

KAY. *(holding up flute)* What about Dudley?

MICHAEL. What about Dudley?

KAY. Aren't you going to find him?

MICHAEL. What for?

KAY. He's your date, isn't he?

MICHAEL. So?

KAY. So, shouldn't he be going with us, wherever we're going?

MICHAEL. You mean I'm supposed to go and find him?

KAY. Well?

MICHAEL. And get the reputation that I run after boys? No thank you. If anyone's going to do any running, it's going to be Dudley Harris.

KAY. Sounds familiar.

MICHAEL. I don't know what you mean.

KAY. You do so.

MICHAEL. I do not.

KAY. Do so!

MICHAEL. Do not!

KAY. So!

MICHAEL. Not!

END OF PLAY

www.ingramcontent.com/pod-product-compliance
Lightning Source LLC
Chambersburg PA
CBHW071844290426
44109CB00017B/1915